...bled Treasures:
...d Heritage Sites

PYRAMIDS OF EGYPT

Cynthia Kennedy Henzel

ABDO Publishing Company

visit us at
www.abdopublishing.com

Published by ABDO Publishing Company, 8000 West 78th Street, Edina, Minnesota 55439. Copyright © 2011 by Abdo Consulting Group, Inc. International copyrights reserved in all countries. No part of this book may be reproduced in any form without written permission from the publisher. The Checkerboard Library™ is a trademark and logo of ABDO Publishing Company.

Printed in the United States of America, North Mankato, Minnesota.
102010
012011

 PRINTED ON RECYCLED PAPER

Cover Photo: Getty Images
Interior Photos: Alamy pp. 5, 27; Corbis pp. 11, 23; Emory Kristof / National Geographic Stock p. 1;
    Getty Images pp. 17, 19, 25; H.M. Herget / National Geographic Stock p. 22;
    iStockphoto pp. 4, 13, 26; Peter Arnold p. 13; Photolibrary pp. 8, 14–15, 29;
    Victor R. Boswell Jr. / National Geographic Stock p. 21

Series Coordinator: BreAnn Rumsch
Editors: Heidi M.D. Elston, BreAnn Rumsch
Art Direction & Cover Design: Neil Klinepier

Library of Congress Cataloging-in-Publication Data

Henzel, Cynthia Kennedy, 1954-
  Pyramids of Egypt / Cynthia Kennedy Henzel.
      p. cm.
  Includes index.
  ISBN 978-1-61613-566-9
  1. Pyramids--Egypt--Juvenile literature. I. Title.
  DT63.H46 2011
  932--dc22
                                   2010021308

CONTENTS

Thousands of years ago, amazing structures called pyramids were built in Egypt. They served as tombs for the country's kings, or pharaohs. The greatest were constructed during the Old Kingdom. This period in Egypt's history is also known as the Pyramid Age.

In ancient times, polished white limestone covered the pyramids. These buildings shone brightly in the hot desert sand. They were symbols of light, representing sunbeams.

Today, much of the white limestone is gone. These dull stone pyramids hardly look like sunbeams. Yet, they shed light on Egypt's amazing and mysterious past. Scientists study these structures to understand ancient Egyptians.

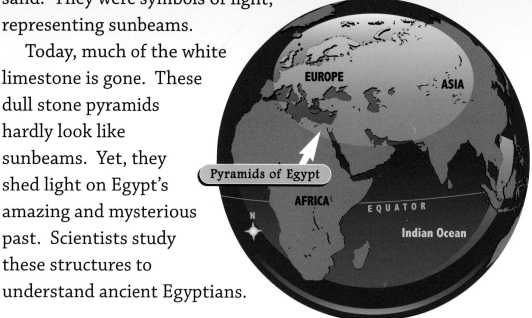

Pyramids of Egypt

There are dozens of pyramids in Egypt. The largest are at Giza. This is near the ancient city of Memphis. The Giza Pyramids were built more than 4,600 years ago.

UNESCO officials recognized the worldwide importance of Egypt's pyramids by naming them a World Heritage site. This will help preserve these mysterious wonders for years to come.

Egypt's pyramids rise from the desert like giants.

Journey to the Afterlife

Ancient Egyptians believed in the afterlife, or life after death. They believed they would journey to a new world after they died.

The Egyptians would need their bodies for this new life. So after death, they were preserved through mummification. This process had several steps. It took many days to complete.

First, the brain and other organs were removed. However, the heart remained. The stomach, intestines, lungs, and liver were preserved in special jars. Next, the body was preserved with chemicals. Then, it was wrapped in cloth and placed in a **coffin**. Finally, the mummy was laid to rest.

A pharaoh's coffin was placed in a pyramid. The organ jars were placed there, too. Food, water, and personal belongings were also provided. These items would help the pharaoh's spirit on its long journey.

More to Explore
Ancient Egyptians connected the west with death. So, they built their pyramids on the west bank of the Nile River.

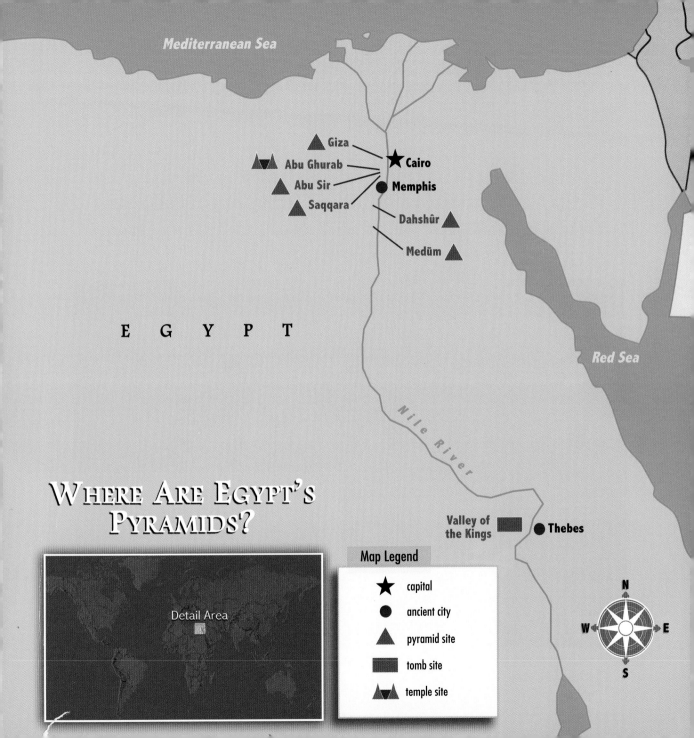

Mediterranean Sea

Giza

Abu Ghurab

Abu Sir

Saqqara

★ Cairo

● Memphis

Dahshûr

Medūm

E G Y P T

Red Sea

Nile River

WHERE ARE EGYPT'S PYRAMIDS?

Detail Area

Valley of the Kings

● Thebes

Map Legend

★ capital

● ancient city

▲ pyramid site

▬ tomb site

▰ temple site

N
W — E
S

Today, Egypt's pyramids seem alone in a sea of sand. Yet originally, each was just one part of a large group of buildings. Smaller pyramids were built near the main ones. These served as tombs for queens of the pharaohs.

Egyptian tomb decorations show many daily activities, such as making bread.

Egypt's Famous Pyramids

In ancient Egypt, pharaohs scattered the desert with pyramids. Some of these early leaders left behind what have become Egypt's most famous pyramids.

PYRAMID	HEIGHT	PHARAOH	REIGN	DYNASTY
Step Pyramid	196.5 feet (60 m)	Djoser	2630–2611 BC	Third
Medūm Pyramid	302 feet (92 m)	Snefru	2575–2551 BC	Fourth
Bent Pyramid	345 feet (105 m)	Snefru		
Red Pyramid	345 feet (105 m)	Snefru		
Great Pyramid	481.4 feet (147 m)	Khufu	2551–2528 BC	Fourth
Khafre's pyramid	471 feet (143 m)	Khafre	2520–2494 BC	Fourth
Menkaure's pyramid	218 feet (66 m)	Menkaure	2490–2472 BC	Fourth
Unas's pyramid	141 feet (43 m)	Unas	2356–2323 BC	Fifth

Near most pyramids, there were two temples connected by a long stone **causeway**. Houses sheltered priests, government officials, guards, and the royal family. Rectangular tombs were built for family members and royal officials.

Building a pyramid required thousands of workers. During construction, a pyramid work site often grew into a town. Skilled builders had workshops on site. And, toolmakers produced supplies for building the pyramid.

All the workers needed clothes, food, and more. So, many others made their living near the pyramid. These included bakers, butchers, sandal makers, doctors, farmers, and pottery makers.

The first known Egyptian pyramid was made for the pharaoh Djoser. He ruled from 2630 to 2611 BC, during Egypt's Third **Dynasty**.

Construction took place at Saqqara. Workers used stone blocks to build the pyramid. In the past, tombs had been made with sun-dried earth bricks.

Workers added many other buildings around the pyramid. The whole area took up 37 acres (15 ha). At the time, this was the size of a large town!

Unlike a true pyramid, Djoser's tomb does not have smooth sides. And at the top, the sides do not meet in a point. The stone blocks were stacked together to form tall slabs. Outer slabs were made shorter than inner slabs. The slabs leaned against one another to create steps. So, this tomb is called the Step Pyramid.

Three and a half miles (5.7 km) of tunnels and rooms run below ground! A central tunnel goes down 92 feet (28 m). It leads to the stone room where Djoser was buried.

At the time it was built, the Step Pyramid was Egypt's largest building.

In 2575 BC, Snefru became the first pharaoh of the Fourth **Dynasty**. His reign began the Pyramid Age. Snefru was Egypt's greatest pyramid builder. Four large tombs were built for him. Just three of them still stand.

The first was built at Medūm. It was made as a step pyramid. However, the steps were later filled in to create smooth sides. Today, much of the Medūm Pyramid has collapsed.

The second pyramid was at Dahshûr. It is bigger than the first. It also has smooth walls, but they are very steep. Halfway up, the angle becomes less steep. This change makes the walls look bent. So, it is called the Bent Pyramid.

Snefru had another tomb built at Dahshûr. It was the first true pyramid with smooth, straight sides. This structure's walls are angled like the top of the Bent Pyramid. Today, its reddish limestone center is exposed. So, it is known as the Red Pyramid.

The Bent Pyramid

In Egypt, no two pyramids are exactly alike. And, no two were built exactly the same way.

The Red Pyramid

The Medūm Pyramid

From 2551 to 2528 BC, Khufu ruled as the second pharaoh of the Fourth **Dynasty**. During this time, the Great Pyramid was constructed at Giza.

The Great Pyramid is the largest ever built. Its entrance is on the north side about 59 feet (18 m) above ground. From there, a tunnel leads down to a chamber 98 feet (30 m) underground.

Another tunnel heads up to the Queen's Chamber. Scientists think this room once held a statue of Khufu.

The same tunnel continues on to the Grand Gallery. This tall hallway travels upward 151 feet (46 m) to

The Great Pyramid (left) may look small in the desert. However, its base originally covered more than 13 acres (5 ha)! Next to it stand Khafre's pyramid (middle) and Menkaure's pyramid (right).

the middle of the tomb. There in the King's Chamber, Khufu was laid to rest. The room is lined with red granite.

Mysterious air shafts lead from the upper chambers to the outside. Some scientists believe they relate to the afterlife. They were meant to lead the pharaoh's spirit out of the tomb.

For centuries, people have studied how the ancient Egyptians completed the Great Pyramid. It remains one of the world's largest buildings.

Most scientists believe the project required 20,000 to 30,000 workers. These men had no strong metal tools. They did not even have **pulleys** to help lift heavy loads. Still, they moved more than 2,300,000 limestone blocks. Each weighed an average of 2.5 tons (2.3 t)!

The Great Pyramid's center is made of local yellow limestone. White limestone covered the inner passages and the outer walls. This stone came from east of the Nile River. The red granite was brought from 580 miles (934 km) away!

The wonders don't stop there. The Egyptians did not have compasses. Yet, the Great Pyramid's walls face almost perfectly north and south. The Egyptians did not have modern **levels** either. Still, the building's base sits flat and even.

More to Explore
A piece of stone called a pyramidion topped each pyramid. At Giza, these stones may have been covered with gold!

Most tunnels in the Great Pyramid are small. However, the Grand Gallery is 26 feet (8 m) high!

Two more major pyramids were built at Giza during the Fourth **Dynasty**. One was constructed for the pharaoh Khafre. He ruled from 2520 to 2494 BC.

Khafre's pyramid is smaller than the Great Pyramid. It is famous for the Great Sphinx nearby. This giant statue has the body of a lion and the head of a man. The Sphinx was carved from the limestone where it sits.

Scientists have many ideas about why the Sphinx was built. A temple sits at its front paws. So, some believe it was built for sun worship. Others think it guards a hidden passage. But, none has ever been discovered.

The blowing desert sands have covered the Sphinx several times. Over the years, the statue has become heavily eroded. Its beard and nose fell off many centuries ago. Recently, it has undergone major repairs.

The third main pyramid at Giza was built for Menkaure. He ruled from 2490 to 2472 BC. Menkaure's pyramid was made smaller than the other two Giza Pyramids. However, its temples were larger and had more costly decorations.

The Great Sphinx is 66 feet (20 m) tall and 240 feet (73 m) long. It seems to guard Khafre's pyramid.

Egypt's Fifth **Dynasty** began in 2465 BC. At Abu Sir, pharaohs built several pyramids. These were poorly made, but their temples were beautifully decorated. The pyramid builders also created sun temples nearby. Two survive today at Abu Ghurab.

Unas reigned from 2356 to 2323 BC. He was the last pharaoh of the Fifth Dynasty. He built his pyramid at Saqqara. It is the smallest of any in the Old Kingdom.

The walls of Unas's burial chamber are covered with beautiful, blue **hieroglyphs**. This is the first example of Pyramid Texts in a pharaoh's burial chamber. These writings include prayers, songs, and spells. They were meant to help the pharaoh on his journey to the afterlife.

After the Pyramid Age ended, pharaohs continued to build pyramids for several hundred years. But none were as great as those of the past. In 2040 BC, the Middle Kingdom began. The last royal pyramids were built in this period, during the Seventeenth Dynasty.

Unas's pyramid is decorated with 283 of more than 700 known Pyramid Texts.

Pyramid workers used simple wood and stone tools to create many amazing structures.

Egyptians needed advanced knowledge to build a pyramid. First, they had to plan out the site. Researchers believe the builders did this by measuring stars. A point halfway between where a star rose and set marked north.

Next, workers needed to make the site even and flat. They made a square **level** by joining two sticks at a 90-degree angle. Then, they hung a weight from the middle. The workers wanted the weight to hang exactly between the two sticks. This told them the tool was on even ground.

Workers mined stone by cutting channels into the rock with stone hammers. This separated blocks from the main stone. Wooden **levers** helped remove them. Then, workers moved the blocks by pulling them with ropes. Stones from far away were floated on boats down the Nile River.

Egyptian pyramids were built with huge limestone blocks. It probably took about 20 men to move one block!

Scientists believe the Egyptians built a giant ramp against each pyramid. Then, workers used the ramp to bring up the stones. Levers helped set the stones in place. Skilled workers used copper tools to cut and shape the outer stones. Finally, they polished the limestone until it shone.

By the time Egypt's New Kingdom began in 1550 BC, many pyramids had been robbed. Pharaohs now wanted a more secret burial place for their treasures. So, they began hiding their tombs in a valley. It was on the Nile River's west bank near the ancient city of Thebes. Today, this area is known as the Valley of the Kings.

Over time, many tombs were built there. So far, 62 tombs have been discovered. Some have many rooms that extend far back into the hills. The walls are decorated with images and **hieroglyphs**.

In AD 1922, the tomb of King Tutankhamen was discovered. He had ruled from 1333 to 1323 BC. Tutankhamen's tomb was filled with treasures. And, his mummy was still in its solid-gold **coffin**!

This priceless discovery drew worldwide attention. **UNESCO** recognized the need to preserve Thebes's history. Officials made the area a World Heritage site in 1979. The site includes the Valley of the Kings.

More to Explore
Near the Valley of the Kings lies the Valley of the Queens. It contains the tombs of queens and princes of the New Kingdom.

Tutankhamen's tomb became famous for its riches. The four rooms were filled with gold objects, jewelry, clothes, furniture, weapons, and other treasures.

Egypt's pyramids have stood in the blowing sand for thousands of years. Some have collapsed. Others have been buried over time.

The pyramids have also been damaged by people. Long ago, many outer blocks were taken to use for other buildings. Tomb robbers dug into the sides seeking treasure. Some even used explosives to get into these grand buildings.

Today, Egypt works to protect what is left of its past. Still, the pyramids remain in danger. Development in the city of Cairo has caused

The Giza Pyramids are one of the Seven Wonders of the Ancient World. Today, they are the only one left.

Ancient builders tried to make the pyramids difficult to invade. Today, steps and railings help visitors safely tour these treasures.

flooding. This threatens the pyramids and other ancient treasures. Water leaves salt on the limestone. Over time, this salt destroys the stone.

Tourism also threatens the pyramids. Thousands of tourists visit Egypt's ancient sites every day. While inside the pyramids, each person breathes out small amounts of water. As the water dries up, it leaves behind damaging salt.

Egypt is rich in ancient monuments. **UNESCO** officials felt many of these should be protected for future generations. In 1979, they declared the Memphis area a World Heritage site. The site includes the pyramids at Giza, Saqqara, and Dahshûr.

Egypt's government is also working on **conservation** projects. One focus is promoting education about Egypt's history. Another is improving Egypt's museums.

Meanwhile, new rules are in place to protect the pyramids. These include tougher laws against **vandalism** and theft. At Giza, an outer road keeps traffic at a distance.

Limited numbers of people are allowed inside the Giza Pyramids each day. Each year, one closes for cleaning or repairs. Visitors may enter the other two.

Ancient Egyptians believed that "to speak the name of the dead is to make him live again." This great wisdom is reflected by Egypt's pyramids. They remind us of the pharaohs who built them. With care, these treasures will stand for years to come. In this way, the pharaohs will continue to live on.

A tomb in the Valley of the Kings

Our Valuable World Heritage

Around the globe, UNESCO World Heritage sites represent important civilizations and natural places. Cultural sites include historic buildings, towns, and monuments as well as important archaeological sites. Natural sites contain rare species or natural marvels. Or, they provide important examples of Earth's natural processes. Mixed sites share both cultural and natural elements. World Heritage sites protect and promote these global treasures for future generations.

causeway - a long corridor used for traveling between pyramid temples.

coffin - a box or a chest for burying a dead body.

conservation - the planned management of rivers, forests, and other natural resources in order to protect and preserve them. Conservation can also protect man-made resources, such as historic or cultural structures.

dynasty - a series of rulers who belong to the same family.

hieroglyph - a hieroglyphic character. Hieroglyphics is a system of writing with pictures used by ancient Egyptians.

level - an instrument used for showing whether a surface is flat and even.

lever - a bar used to pull apart or move something.

pulley - a wheel over which a rope or a cable may be pulled. It helps move or change the direction of heavy loads.

UNESCO - United Nations Educational, Scientific, and Cultural Organization. A special office created by the United Nations in 1945. It aims to promote international cooperation in education, science, and culture.

vandalism - intentional damage done to public or private property.

Abu Ghurab - ah-boo GOO-rahb
Abu Sir - ah-boo SEER
Dahshûr - dah-SHUR
Djoser - ZHOH-suhr
Giza - GEE-zuh
hieroglyph - HEYE-ruh-glihf
Khafre - KAF-ray
Khufu - KOO-foo
Medūm - meh-DOOM

Memphis - MEHM-fuhs
Menkaure - mehn-KOW-ray
pharaoh - FEHR-oh
Saqqara - suh-KAHR-uh
Snefru - SNEHF-roo
Thebes - THEEBZ
Tutankhamen - too-tang-KAHM-uhn
Unas - OO-nuhs

WEB SITES

To learn more about the Pyramids of Egypt, visit
ABDO Publishing Company online. Web sites about the Pyramids of Egypt
are featured on our Book Links page. These links are routinely monitored
and updated to provide the most current information available.
www.abdopublishing.com

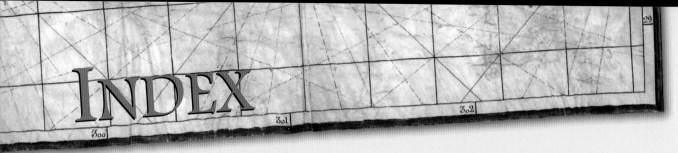

Index